MANIFESTING MY SELFHOOD IN CERÁMICA

MANIFESTING MY SELFHOOD IN CERÁMICA

BRIAN S. HEFFERNAN

PALMETTO
PUBLISHING
Charleston, SC
www.PalmettoPublishing.com

Paperback ISBN: 979-8-8229-5660-5

My Sincerest Dedication

To my deceased Grandma and Grandpa Jorth for giving me such a wonderful childhood in Ceylon, Minnesota whenever I came out to visit with my family. Thank you Grandma Jorth for "*The Illustrated Book of Fairy Tales*" retold by Neil Philip, to keep my imagination active and alive.

To the Girón family, thank you so much for everything you have done for me and my family the past twenty-three years. Thanks for all the love, gifts, home cooked meals, sleepovers and birthday celebrations!

To my dad who taught me what it means to be an artist and how to live my life to my full potential. Thanks so much for accompanying Mom and I to see my favorite film adaptation of "*Alice In Wonderland*" in 2010. I miss you and wish you could see my success!

To my mom who told me to keep on my feet and look straight ahead when success is so close. Thanks for being the wonderful mom you are and I can't wait to share my Poetry Thesis with you! Thank you for supporting me and putting the time and patience to support me in my major at Columbia College Chicago.

To my therapist Steffeny, for making me a better person the past 5 ½ years!

To my friend Luis Hernandez, I couldn't thank you enough for everything you have taught me since I met you in Mexico City. We are so alike in many ways. I am glad you found comfort in my Poetry, including the poem "Fraternal", that is displayed on your bedroom door. Thank you for being my artistic muse this year when I needed to draw out internalized inspiration for my Thesis. I can't wait to bring my Poetry Thesis to you in the near future when I see you in Mexico City with your mom and grandma again.

Sincerely,
Brian Heffernan

"The mountains may never meet other mountains...
but people will always meet again."

– *Calabrian Proverb*

Contents

[Céramica street 137 is undoubtedly my home]

Céramica street 137 is undoubtedly my home

Your mathematical mind guides me through the labyrinthian

neighborhood

The way we sauntered towards the home was like witnessing

plants budding

a recurring fraternal bond

The ash pink and faded grey home

guarded by a tree out in the front

Within milliseconds I have walked across the door's threshold

My brother's family's thoughts about me evolved like a blood red

sunset disappearing

The home bloomed as a chrysanthemum when my brother and I

began to have conversations

At 11pm, I asked him in my aquatic zone aphotic voice about

"fragility"

He answers back in his accented voice combined with British

English and Mexican dialect, assuring me that he doesn't want to

see me hurt

I have never forgotten the pathos your black eyes expressed

when you stood in the rain

Glass Hyacinth

April 29th Full moon's luster gleams through the rain splattered
window
Pasquale leaned casually against the freshly painted coral window
ledge
He opened the window at five minutes past three in the morning
Gusts of frigid air induced his body to shiver uncontrollably
through the mauve sweater
In his chest, he slowly developed pleuritic symptoms
Now, with the sun rising in the sky, it welcomes another day
Thawed Hyacinths in the garden take in the melted water from
the soil hourly
One single purple Hyacinth stood out in the garden's far distance
Recalling her deep blue eyes in the daylight
He asked himself, "Why was Pasqualina cold towards me before
Easter?"

Saint's Sun

his eyes were pristine and clear
as they held the truth, no matter how bad it was
he would never harm a creature
that lives in darkness, own a calloused soul, possesses a
wounded heart
or one that is born with grotesque beauty
what resided in the saint's heart projected
vulnerability and kindness as blooming rose buds
he was always alone but never hot while trekking through the
sweltering savanna
his compassionate nature emits sunshine
on the last day in the savanna, he swallowed the scorching sun
which killed him
his gentle demeanor became stars at night
inlaid within the sky's galaxy and the creeping aurora borealis
at midnight

[My girlfriend seductively moans in her vestal virgin white dress]

my girlfriend seductively moans in her vestal virgin white dress
whenever she puts the
meat in the
grinder at midnight
to cook me empanadas
at 1am in our
pristine kitchen
that is clean
as a surgical operating room

Dual Alice

Understanding Lewis Carroll's "Alice In Wonderland", and its
character Alice helped me when I was a teenager

at age 15
My civility within biculturalism cannot hide well
Thus, it is like Alice's

Popping antipsychotics throughout childhood altered my body's
weight
My therapist, perched like Absolem on her chair, questioning me

With portioned foods on my white ceramic plate, I fear Macropsia
And Cerebral psychosis

A rusted copper warded barrel key dangles from my neck that
unlocks my innocence
Subversion of my dreams dispels a fortified belief that childhood
is imperishable

You are all late to my Corprolalia hypnotherapy session !!!

Edgewater Area

Eeeeeeeeeeeeeekkkkwwwweeeeee eeeeeeeeeeekkkwwwwwwweeeee – seagulls flying above me. I heard seagulls flying over me at Ostermann Beach in the Edgewater area. I do not find birds beautiful or peaceful. I find them the most annoying animal existing on the planet. When I looked up to see what was flying above me, I felt that I was in Hitchcock's movie, The Birds that stars Tippi Hedren. That movie did traumatize me as I do have phobia of birds. It brought back memories when I would be scared of going to a bird conservatory and I would panic and hyperventilate so much that I would have to be guided with my eyes closed and walk through it in this particular manner. Seeing a seagull above me, it propelled me to channel my phobia of birds into words rather than actions.

Guilty Heart

Alone, sitting on a woven rug next to a scrapbook
I open the vintage anthology
I try to not let the ink on each page get ruined
Your soul is the mirror of a past unrequited action

As winter approaches, I see the iron fence on the horizon
Frozen memories of so many years, I wish I could skate
with them again
In the wind, I can see a beautiful smile I used to know

[When my "5'5" mother argues]

When my "5'5" mother argues, her voice screeches like a
raven, which I capture in various jars. I untwist the jars in the
Caribbean Sea that my mom swims in when we are done with
the phase of diatribe. We watch the jars float away from our feet.
It is a resplendent peacock.

[She lunged on top of a cerulean casket]

She lunged on top of a cerulean casket

which transformed into a worn bed with broken coils

the inner child that resides within me tugs my wailing mother

as the mossy blanket absorbs her tears

Time stood still, time stood still

and

faded

A Hundred Thousand Hours: Poem for April 5th

My anesthetized secular thoughts ricocheted against the church's

stained-glass window.

Virgin Mary's bust is my staring mother, still and motionless.

The cross dangles mid-air and lurches down the fragmented

worn wooden aisle.

Swinging black rosary knocks off vases of twisted white

chrysanthemums bestowed by my mother on Jesus's altar.

[Because the rain that falls on my raincoat]

Because the rain falls on my raincoat it acts as an
emotional release
Because of this rain, I do a lonely waltz, humming the
music to myself
Because of this dance I did at 9 pm yesterday, pneumonia
crept into my lungs
Because of this illness, I am bedridden and the flowers next
to my bed are always upright and fresh looking
Because of the fresh daffodils that are next to my bed,
they trigger memories of buying flowers at a farmer's
market as a child
Because of this memory, my strength helped me recover as
I hobbled from my bed to the clear bedroom window
Because I'm able to walk and not lie in my bed, I can
watch the sunset that turns in various shades of blazing
yellow before setting behind the mountains

[*Whenever I speak, I don't know why it has an aphotic*]

Whenever I speak, I don't know why it has an aphotic tone

Can someone tell me why I am ambiguous in looks?

I don't understand the transition of hair follicles from fine

to coarse

Why do people insist I possess my mother's eyes?

I wonder if knowledge is passed down or acquired

Does my temper come from the Tyrrhenian Sea or the

Caribbean Sea?

Is my mindset slow in the winter but fast in the summer?

Is reclusiveness hereditary or picked up environmentally?

Are my dark eyes beady, expressive, or just a blank void in

the eye sockets?

[*A lightless night without the basking sun*]

A lightless night without the basking sun

A Cimmerian night where the sky is rose colored

A Candlelit night where it's generated by kerosene flames

A morose day without feelings that is unrequited

A lurid day where the nightmare caused internal hallucinations

A gorgonian day where the suicide attempt was frightening

A rain made of dried forest fire leaves

A rain made of molten black needles

A rain made of ceramic marbles

[whenever i travel my personal traumas]

whenever i travel

my personal traumas

    are at ease

    as they slip

    into a language performance

        it becomes chameleonic

        and worn in

            like a vintage leather shoe

            that hides back

            in a dusty closet

                neurologically, brain and throat

                communicate to send verbose messages

                which come out with a slight accent and precision

[Understanding Lewis Carroll's, "Alice In Wonderland", and its character Alice helped me with my metamorphosis during my teenage years – 4 things about me]

Understanding Lewis Carroll's, "Alice In Wonderland", and its character Alice helped me with my metamorphosis during my teenage years

Street 137 on Céramica is undoubtedly my home

Physically being an airline passenger gave a sense of welcoming adrenaline and openness

Holding passports allows me to slip into the mother tongue's culture

[I said learn How chlorophyll fills]

I said learn

How chlorophyll fills

The green leaves

During the springtime

As I plucked off a crisp, cool leaf

Off the hanging tree branch

That rubbed against my head

Its hard bark became

Stuck in my short cropped hair

I pulled out the bark that became

Dried and broke into halves on

My calloused hand, which I washed

My hand in water with the bark

Its texture felt grainy against my hand

It felt as if it was a pumice Stone

Washing and stripping away grime

And sap from the decaying tree

Where its ring circles of life

Indicates it is a thousand years old

More leaves began to bud

During the downpour of rain and thunder

Everyday, I see leaf buds the size of a quarter blooming

into a full sized leaf

Illustrious Walk

The forest tree caving in the way

During the Springtime of the spirits

Sunlight ceasing

From the hilltop it speaks of their story

They are young and their life is a long road: those we love

Yet it is difficult to say bye to you

Retracing steps like the old time

Standing next to the glistening lake

Watching tulip petals fly in the wind

Reunite

In my heart, an archaic poem is strung together

As I wait outside in the wind for this Gallic girl

6.07pm Ostermann Beach

1. Lakefront water- idyllic
2. Quiet
3. Barren and dry environment
4. Warmth of the sun
5. Looks like the area is ready for Spring

1) Pfffffttttt cccccccccccsssssshhhhh ccccccccccccccccccccssssssssshhhhh –noise of the water crashing the lakefront edges.
2) Eeeeeeeeeeeeeekkkkkwwwwweeeeee eeeeeeeeeeekkkkww-wwwwweeeee – seagulls flying above me.
3) 6.07pm Ostermann beach

[City walk part 1]

City walk part 1

i see the curved street
with two tall structures

rustic Train cars elevated
above worn parking lot

metallic, phallic looking building
in the horizon

graphic grey pasted on red building
above parking lot

shriveled dried black leaves
rustling in the wind as symphonic sounds

sky blue meets white bridge
passerby underneath

aligned trees like dominoes with leaves
beckoned to the wind

cloudy sky with sunshine
rising above buildings
looks like a Monet painting

reflective mirrors shine dry trees and sky
as I walk by it
a reflective panel looks back at me

as I draw close by
i see darkness
greyness
and limber trees, motionless

[City walk part 2]

came halfway to
a bridge, a road
and aligned lamps
with sunshine glaring

as I gaze far
towards the horizon
i see a fountain
and
hear motors

[Cold water drops ran over me as I stood under the showerhead]

Cold water drops ran over me as I stood under the showerhead

My mind is crisp and clear

My body shivers in the cold

As I push back the curtain to get the towel

Frigid air hits me as if snow has stuck on me

I wrap myself in a faded off-white towel with my name

embroidered in green

Thursday's Midnight

Standing in the bleak morning   1am   Electrical

lamps

   Shine gilded yellow.   Yawning and

   Relaxing against the

     Cold iron streetlight exhaling condensation   turning

into bats

Soaring towards the stars

Which perch on   decayed branches

Resting peacefully and swaying   in moonshadow

That shows nocturnal eyes.

Pffffftttt cccccccccccssssshhhhh
cccccccccccccccccccsssssssssshhhhh –noise of the water crashing
the lakefront edges. I walked for several blocks on along the
lakefront in Edgewater to get to Ostermann beach. Even
though I can hear the cold water splashing on the concrete
edge of the lakefront path, my right ear hears the hum of the
wave crashing on the lakefront concrete pathway. I stood
where the benches were and just stood still gazing at the
lakefront, sometimes the water, the cold air hitting my face.
I didn't have gloves on for this outdoor activity. My hands
became numb and rigid so I put them in my pants pockets.
I wanted to go stand at the pier on Ostermann Beach but it
was too dangerous. The water was crashing all over the pier's
pathway and I didn't want to stand there and slip.

Riddle Violin

The forest trees caving in the way, a mystery for one who listens
to the mind, soul, and wind Falls on his knees in this dirtied
path in confusion

Around you, you must mind and heed
A lantern in the darkness, I question "why"
Where should I go or should I continue or stop

Smile a Mile

Walking along the lake, thinking of what I can do in my wildest time
Looking at the sky within the stars, inlaid in the night sky

The road continues ahead
Could the darkness blind my dreams, or could the light shield
me from it
Close your eyes, look down deep, into your soul

You can walk through dreams for endless miles
As a fragmented world
I could walk through my life in the dark